Rip!

By Jacinta Hayden

Library For All Ltd.

Rip!

First published 2023

Published by Library For All Ltd
Email: info@libraryforall.org
URL: libraryforall.org

Our Yarning logo design by Jason Lee, Bidjipidji Art

Original illustrations by Fariza Dzatalin Nurtsani

Rip!
Hayden, Jacinta
ISBN: 978-1-923110-44-1
SKU03343

Rip!

We respect and honour Aboriginal and Torres Strait Islander Elders past, present and future. We acknowledge the stories, traditions and living cultures of Aboriginal and Torres Strait Islander peoples on this land and commit to building a brighter future together.

I like to swim at the beach.

Mum says don't go out
of reach.

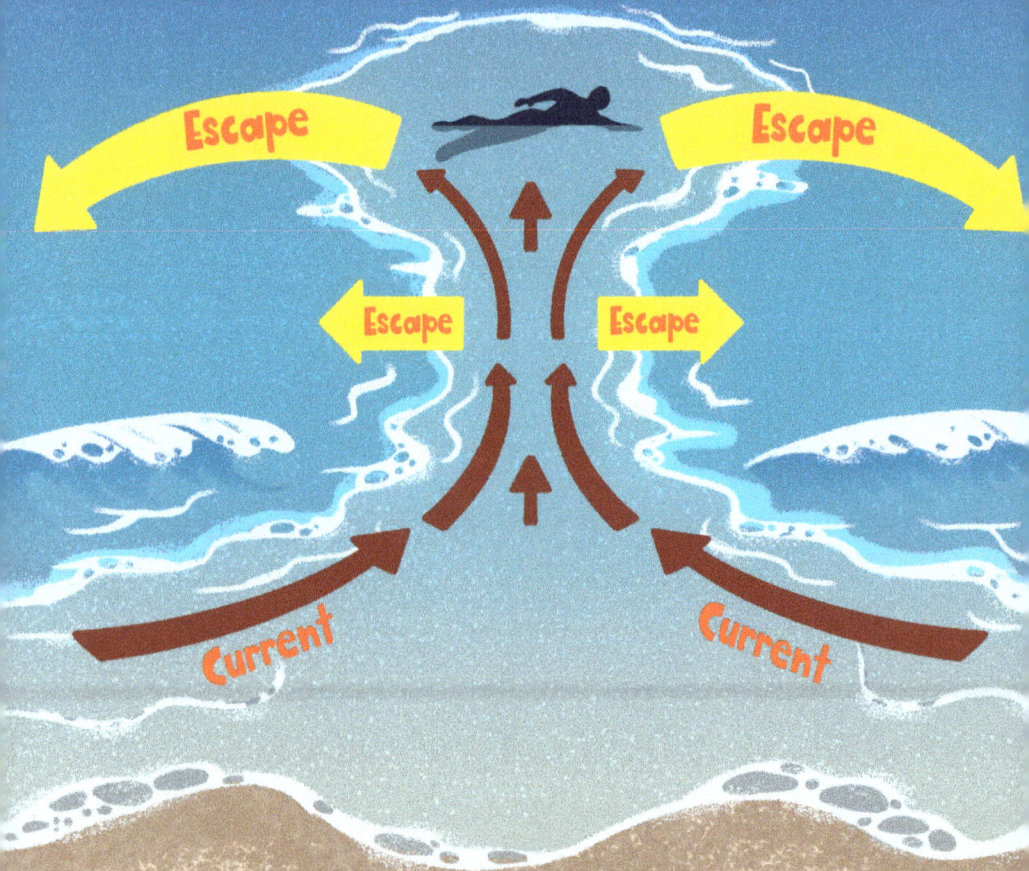

Rip Currents

Escape

Escape

Escape

Escape

Current

Current

She's worried I'll get caught in a rip.

That would be a scary dip.

I know to keep my head
up high.

Keep looking at the clear
blue sky.

Relax and, when the current
is not so strong,

wave my arms, calmly kick,
and float along.

Incoming waves

Rip head

Incoming waves

Swim parallel to shore

Rip channel

Direction
of current

Beach

Swim along the shore,
not out to sea.

Safe in shallow waters,
you soon will be.

You can use these questions to talk about this book with your family, friends and teachers.

What did you learn from this book?

Describe this book in one word. Funny? Scary? Colourful? Interesting?

How did this book make you feel when you finished reading it?

What was your favourite part of this book?

download our reader app
getlibraryforall.org

About the author

Jacinta is from the Whadjuk/Noongar Nation. She grew up in Merredin and now lives in Perth. She loves to yarn and share stories. When she was young, she loved the book *Green Eggs and Ham*.

Darwin

NORTHERN
TERRITORY

QUEENSLAND

WESTERN
AUSTRALIA

SOUTH
AUSTRALIA

Brisbane

NEW SOUTH
WALES

Perth

Adelaide

Sydney

ACT
Canberra

Author's Country

VICTORIA
Melbourne

TASMANIA
Hobart

Our Yarning

Want to discover more books from this collection?
Our Yarning is a collection of books written by
Aboriginal and Torres Strait Islander peoples
across Australia.

We know that children learn better, and enjoy
reading more, when they see themselves in the
stories, characters and illustrations of the books
they read.

To download the app, visit the Google Play Store
on any Android device and search 'Our Yarning'.

libraryforall.org